21st Cent
SKILLS LIBR

.S.
NS

VOTING DAY

by
Samantha
Bell

Cherry Lake Press

Cherry Lake Press

Published in the United States of America by
Cherry Lake Publishing Group
Ann Arbor, Michigan
www.cherrylakepublishing.com

Reading Adviser: Beth Walker Gambro, MS, Ed., Reading Consultant, Yorkville, IL

Content Adviser: Mark Richards, Ph.D., Professor, Dept. of Political Science, Grand Valley State University, Allendale, MI

Photo Credits: © Burlingham/Shutterstock, cover, title page; © Karin Hildebrand Lau/Shutterstock, 5; © Agable/Shutterstock, 7; © Niyazz/Shutterstock, 8; © Krakenimages.com/Shutterstock, 9; © Lisa F. Young/Shutterstock, 10; © Red Herring/Shutterstock, 13; © Josie Elias/Shutterstock, 14; © Sharkshock/ Shutterstock, 15; © SeventyFour/Shutterstock, 16; © Dragon Images/Shutterstock, 17; © Trevor Bexon/Shutterstock, 18; © JHDT Productions/Shutterstock, 21; © Gorodenkoff/Shutterstock, 23; © Lisa F. Young/Shutterstock, 24; © Gorodenkoff/Shutterstock, 25; © John Kershner/Shutterstock, 26; © bluestork/ Shutterstock, 29; © Rosamar/Shutterstock, 30; © Linda Parton/Shutterstock, 31; © Trevor Bexon/Shutterstock, 32; © Johnny Silvercloud/Shutterstock, 33; Florida State Archives, 34; ElizabethForMA, CC BY 2.0 via Wikimedia Commons, 37; Voice of America, Public domain, via Wikimedia Commons, 38; Xackery Irving/ Shutterstock, 39; © chaylek/Shutterstock, 41; © Rob Crandall/Shutterstock, 42; © 24K-Production/Shutterstock, 43

Cherry Lake Press is an imprint of Cherry Lake Publishing Group.

Library of Congress Cataloging-in-Publication Data has been filed and is available at catalog.loc.gov

Printed in the United States of America

Note from Publisher: Websites change regularly, and their future contents are outside of our control. Supervise children when conducting any recommended online searches for extended learning opportunities.

CONTENTS

CHAPTER 1

POLLING PLACES

A polling place is where people go to vote in local, state, and federal elections. In U.S. elections, most votes are cast inside polling places. Voters choose their preferred candidate by marking a **ballot** at the polling place.

A person's polling place is based on where they live. State or local election officials decide where the polling places will be. People must vote at their assigned polling place. The location may change from one election to the next.

TYPES OF POLLING PLACES

The location of polling places depends on state laws. Some states are more specific than others. Polling places are usually public buildings. This is because they are more familiar to voters. They also

A variety of different locations can serve as polling places in a community. A polling place must be accessible to people with disabilities.

meet the requirements of the Americans with Disabilities Act. This act protects voters with disabilities. It requires that state and local governments make sure they have the same opportunity to vote.

Public schools may serve as polling places. Some states require that schools used as polling places close for the day. In some cities, all public schools are closed on Election Day anyway. The school district may make it a school holiday or a virtual learning day. Some polling places are located on college or university campuses.

Other buildings in the community can serve as polling places. These include fire stations, police stations, and churches. Senior living centers or residences are also often used.

Some states don't specify any type of polling place location. They have no restrictions. In these states, election officials can be creative with their choice of locations. They just have to meet the federal and state government requirements. These include accessibility for disabled people. They also involve

Laundromats are often central places in a community. The Su Nueva Laundromat in Chicago has been one of the most unusual polling locations in recent years.

parking space availability, size of the premises, and distance between the voting machines.

The officials who choose polling place locations take other things into consideration. They want people to feel safe in the voting area. They also think about where the polling place is located in the community. Some unusual locations have included a bowling alley, a laundromat, a laboratory, and a farmer's garage!

Colorado led the way with centralized vote centers. Vote centers can make it easier for people to vote.

Voters should check where their polling place is before Election Day. They can't change their polling location. If they move, they must change their address on their voter registration. That way, they can be assigned a new polling place near their new home.

Some states have also created vote centers. At a vote center, any voter within the **jurisdiction** can vote. It does not matter what their address or assigned **precinct** is. Colorado was the first state to use vote centers in 2003. Today, 18 states currently allow people to use vote centers on Election Day.

POLL WORKERS

A poll worker is someone who helps at the polls on Election Day. They have many important responsibilities. They help make sure that elections are free and fair.

Poll workers start early in the day. The hours when polling places are open vary by state. Many are open from 7:00 a.m. to 7:00 p.m. Poll workers must arrive much earlier. They have to set up and prepare the

Poll workers are an essential part of the voting process.

Voters in many states insert their ballots into optical scan voting machines. These machines scan the ballots to count votes.

polling location. They have to get the voting machines ready.

During the election, a team of poll workers keeps everything running smoothly. They welcome voters and direct them to the voting area. Then they verify voters' registrations and issue ballots. They make sure voters know how to use the voting equipment. They explain how to mark the ballot. They answer any questions. They make sure the ballots are collected properly.

People who want to be poll workers must meet certain requirements. These vary by state. Many states require that poll workers be at least 18 years old. Usually, they have to live in the same county as the polling place. Training is provided, and many states pay the poll workers. Some poll workers work half a day. Others work the whole day. They all help serve their communities.

PERSPECTIVES: ELECTIONEERING

Electioneering includes signs and written or spoken words that try to sway a voter's opinion. It is illegal for people to electioneer in or near polling places. It can unfairly influence other voters. It is a serious offense.

For this reason, voters at the polls can't wear clothing or buttons with a candidate's slogan. They can't make comments about a candidate or party. Electioneering also includes bumper stickers and campaign signs that are too close to the polling place. Poll workers should also avoid discussing anything political. They should always try to be aware of what is going on in the polling location.

CHAPTER 2

VOLUNTEERS

Elections run more smoothly when citizens get involved. There are many ways for people to volunteer on Election Day. Many poll workers are paid. But people can also volunteer to be poll workers. Approximately 1 million people are needed to work at the polls.

There are other ways to volunteer. Some volunteers make sure other voters can vote. Some help make sure the election is fair. Volunteers work hard to make sure every vote counts.

HELPING OTHERS

Everyone should be able to exercise their right to vote. Some people volunteer to make this easier for others. For example, some voters have difficulties getting to

Poll workers also make sure absentee ballots are collected and counted with in-person votes.

Some volunteers help educate the elderly or disabled on how to vote. They also make sure voting is accessible.

the polls. They may be elderly or disabled. They may have a hard time getting around. They may not have a car to drive or money for gas. They may not have public transportation in their area. Or they may not feel safe using it.

Volunteers help them by providing transportation. They work with organizations to get the voters to the polls. They pick up the voters in their car. Then they take them to vote. The volunteers may wait for voters there. Or they may pick them up again later to take them home.

Volunteers can't wear clothing or buttons that support a certain candidate. They don't talk to the voters about the issues. Their goal is not to support

Some polling places offer curbside voting for disabled and elderly voters.

a party. It's just to help people get to the polling place.

Other volunteers help out at the polls. Many times, polling places need volunteers who are bilingual. Sometimes voters come in who don't speak English well. They don't understand the poll worker's directions. The volunteers serve as **interpreters**.

Poll workers can have a hard time communicating instructions. The interpreters fill in the gap. Without them, voters may become discouraged. They may leave the polling place without voting.

People who speak other languages are a great asset at polling places.

Election observers work to keep the election fair for everyone.

KEEPING IT FAIR

Some **nonpartisan** organizations train volunteers to observe elections. These are called nonpartisan observers. The organizations and volunteers are not connected with a political party. They go to the polls to watch the election. They are not focused on a party or candidate. They are working only to make sure the election is honest and fair. After the election, they will often write reports with their observations. They might also recommend how future elections could be improved.

Poll watchers are similar to nonpartisan observers. They also volunteer to **monitor** the polls. But they are appointed by their political party.

Vote-by-mail ballots must also be counted by volunteers. Poll watchers and nonpartisan observers watch this process.

Poll watchers watch over the casting and the counting of ballots in elections. They want to make sure the election is fair for their party.

Each state decides who can be a poll watcher and what they can do on Election Day. They watch as people come to vote. They keep track of the number of voters. But they may not interfere with the voting process. If a poll watcher sees a problem, they must report it to authorities and party officials.

TRUE STORY: A LIFE OF SERVICE

Laura Wooten was born in 1920. That was the same year women won the right to vote. At age 19, she began serving as a poll worker. She believed people should vote every chance they could. It was the only way to see things change.

Wooten volunteered at local, primary, and general election polls in New Jersey. She served as a poll worker for 79 years. She worked on her last Election Day in 2018. She died in 2019 at age 98. She was the longest-serving election poll worker in history.

CHAPTER 3

VOTING DAY

Before someone goes to vote, they can look at a sample ballot. Some states and **nonprofit** organizations provide sample ballots. Voters can also find them online. They can use the sample ballots to help them decide who to vote for. Sample ballots list the names of all the candidates. They also include the offices the candidates are running for. Sample ballots may list state or local issues that are up for a vote. The sample ballot will often look like a real one. That way, voters know what to expect when they go to the polls.

Voters can also read voter guides. These provide even more information. They provide information about the candidates. They give details about their experience. They also explain other things that are on the ballot. These include questions or proposals people can vote on. Voter guides are available in local newspapers or online.

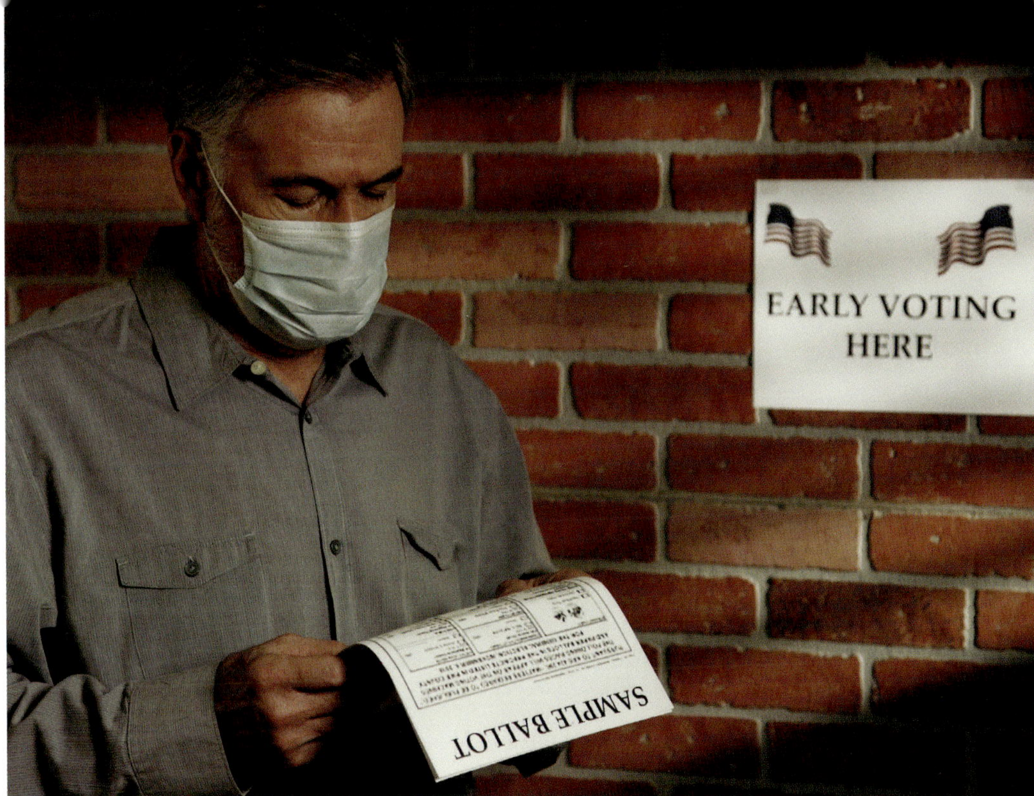

When voters fill out sample ballots ahead of time, it can speed up the voting process.

Voters may print a copy of the sample ballot and voter guide. They may bring both to the polls when they vote. They may also bring any notes about the candidates. That way, they don't have to memorize all of their choices. This can make the voting process easier. Voters should bring paper copies. Some polling places don't allow voters to use cell phones.

TO THE POLLS

Voters can go to the polls anytime they are open. Many people go early in the morning before work. Lunchtime and late afternoon are also popular times. People get in a line with other voters. When it is their turn, a poll worker will ask them their name. The poll worker has a list of registered voters for that precinct. These lists are called rosters. Poll workers make sure each voter is on the roster. Some states use electronic poll books. Others use paper rosters.

There are several reasons a voter may not appear on the list. The voter's registration might have the wrong address. Their name might be misspelled. Or a ballot has already been recorded in the voter's name.

Whatever the reason, the voter can request a provisional ballot. They use this ballot to vote. The ballot will be held until the voter has been **verified**. Then their provisional ballot is counted.

Some states require voters to bring some type of identification (ID) with them. This is to prove that they are the voter on the roster. The states decide what kind of ID is required. Voters may need to bring a driver's license, state ID, or **passport**. Other forms of ID include a voter registration card, a Social Security card, or a birth certificate.

Paper ballots must be filled out with blue or black ink pens.

CASTING THE BALLOT

People can vote in several ways. The states decide which method to use. Different states use different types of voting machines. Some states have several kinds of voting machines.

One method of voting is paper ballots. These ballots list the names of the candidates. Beside each name is a small oval or box. Voters use a pen to fill in the shape next to their preferred candidate. If someone makes a mistake, they can ask for a new ballot. The completed paper ballot is then scanned. The vote is recorded. The ballots may be scanned at the polling place. They may also be scanned at another location. This method of voting is considered the most secure. Paper ballots provide a clear record of each voter's choices. The ballots can be checked and rechecked if necessary.

Another system uses computers. The votes are recorded directly into the computer's memory. Votes can be cast using touchscreens, dials, or buttons. The voter's choices are then stored on a **cartridge** or hard drive. But many security experts think this system

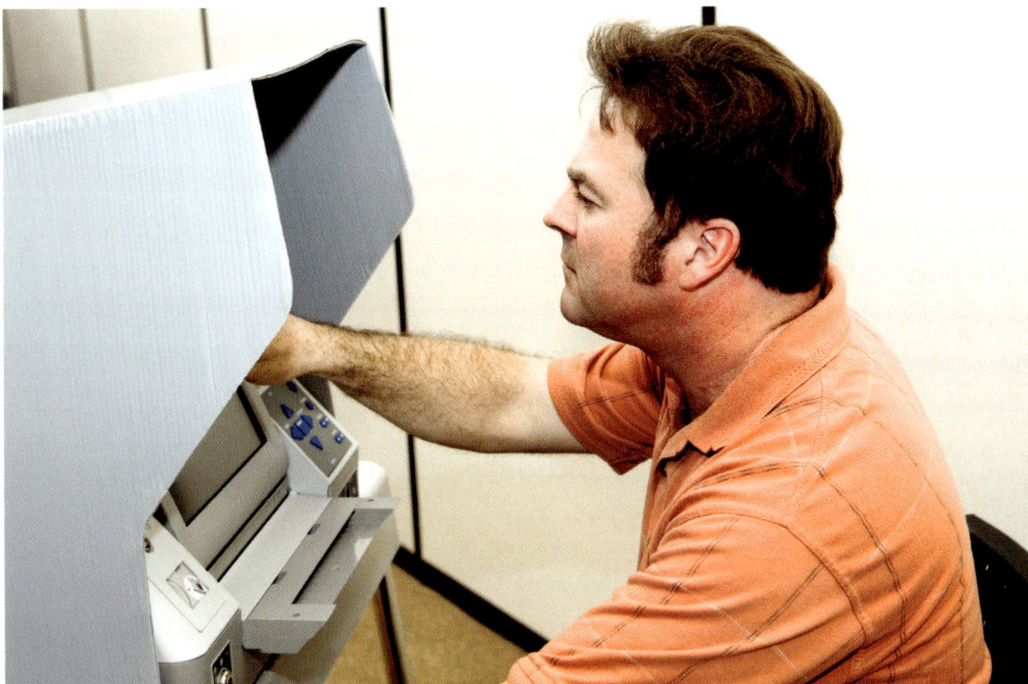

Louisiana is the only state that uses only electronic voting machines. The other states that use them also use other counting methods.

The tried and true paper ballot is still the most private and accurate way to vote.

shouldn't be used. The computers may have software or programming errors. The machines could break down. They could record a vote incorrectly.

A third system is a combination of the other two. The ballot is presented electronically on a computer. The voter makes their selections. Then the computer produces a paper ballot. This ballot shows those selections. The computers don't store any of the information. This system provides paper copies of the ballots. But traditional paper ballots are still the most secure.

Many people choose to vote early. This lets them avoid long wait times at polling places on voting day.

Sometimes the lines to vote are very long. Voters may not be able to vote before closing time. If this happens, voters have the right to stay in line as long as needed. It is their right to cast a ballot. The polling place must stay open.

SPOTLIGHT ON: EARLY VOTING

In recent years, many states have started to provide early voting. This allows people to vote before Election Day. That way, they may not have to wait in long lines. The states choose when they want early voting to begin. It could be a few days or weeks before Election Day. Early voting must be done in person. Usually, voters don't need to provide a reason to vote early.

During early voting, voters can go to a central location. This may be a county office or a vote center. Most vote centers use the same type of voting equipment for early and Election Day voting. Others may use a different method of voting.

CHAPTER 4

COUNTING THE VOTES

Each state determines its own voting rules, laws, and procedures. This includes when the polls open and close on Election Day. Voting is over when the polls close.

After the polls close, local election officials must count and report the votes. Then the results must be verified. This can take days or weeks.

ABSENTEE BALLOTS

Some people are unable to go to the polls on Election Day. They may have a disability, an injury, or an illness. They may be out of town on a business trip or vacation. They may be in college in another city or state. They may be serving in the military.

Absentee ballots can be mailed or dropped in an official ballot drop box.

These voters can still exercise their right to vote. They may send in an absentee ballot. Absentee ballots are also known as mail-in ballots. They allow **eligible** voters to cast their ballots. These voters don't have to go to a polling place. Instead, they vote by mailing in their ballots.

If mailed, some states require absentee ballots to arrive by Election Day.

Some states have permanent absentee voting lists. Voters on this list automatically receive an absentee ballot for each election.

Every state has absentee voting. But the rules for absentee ballots vary. Many states require voters to give a valid reason. These reasons can also vary by state.

Absentee ballots are usually returned by mail. They may also be hand-delivered. For most states, the deadline is Election Day. They must be received by the time the polls close. Some states will count a ballot if it was postmarked on or before Election Day.

Absentee ballots must be processed before they can be counted. This can mean different things in different states. Usually, the first step is to compare signatures. The voter signs the outside of the envelope. Election workers look at the signature. They compare it with the voter's signature on record. They make sure the signatures match. Most states begin processing absentee ballots before the election.

Once the absentee ballots are processed, they may be counted. Counting refers to **tallying** the votes. Most states begin counting absentee ballots on

An election worker examines and counts absentee ballots.

Making sure every vote is counted fairly is an integral part of voting day.

Election Day. Some don't allow counting to start until the polls close.

THE OFFICIAL COUNT

Tallying the votes made in person begins after the polls close. Some states use electronic voting equipment. These ballots are recorded and counted right away. Many states use paper ballots. These must be scanned. The scanner detects the votes. Then it records them electronically.

The Florida Supreme Court ended the hanging chad recount from the 2000 election in December of that year. They decided that Bush had won the popular vote in Florida.

Sometimes a scanner can't read a ballot. It rejects the ballot. An election worker must then process the ballot **manually**.

The equipment used to count the votes is carefully tested and **certified**. Officials make sure it is accurate and secure. The results of the count are added to the state's total tally. This number determines who won the electoral votes for the state.

It can take a long time for the count to be made official. Every ballot must be processed and tallied. This includes all absentee ballots. Protecting the right to vote requires counting every valid ballot.

TRUE STORY: THE HANGING CHAD

In 2000, George W. Bush ran for president against Al Gore. Florida was a swing state in the election. The winner of Florida would become the next president. Soon after the election, the vote tally in Florida showed that Bush was ahead. But the vote was very close. The state had to do a recount. The counting went on for weeks.

Part of the problem was the ballots. They were punch-card ballots. Voters had to punch out a tiny rectangle beside the candidate's name. Sometimes they were not punched all the way. This became known as a "hanging chad." The recount went on. Finally, the Supreme Court ended the recount in December. Bush won Florida. He became president.

CHAPTER 5

DECLARING A WINNER

After the polls close, the media begins posting election results. These trickle in little by little throughout Election Night. The media reports the results as they come in.

Many voters believe that these are the final results. But it can take a long time for all of the votes to be counted and verified. The winner is often announced by the news much sooner. The race is called before the results are official.

EARLY RESULTS

The Associated Press (AP) is a nonprofit news agency. The AP has a long history of counting votes. It began tallying votes in 1848. That year, reporters went all over the country to get the vote totals. They added them to declare the winners. The AP is still one of the most trusted sources for election results.

While the AP reports preliminary results, many people watch expectantly at parties and other gatherings. Senators and state representatives are also waiting to hear if they've been elected.

Today, the AP uses a network of local reporters. The reporters gather results from county clerks and other local officials. First, each precinct counts their votes. Then election workers send the information to county and state officials. Finally, the officials make the counts available to the public. Reporters also gather this information. They get information from state websites. They receive electronic data about the votes as well.

AP reporters send all the information to the AP's vote counting operation. The data is entered into an electronic system. Race callers analyze the data. They know a lot about the states and the candidates. They are experts in election history and rules. They keep track of any changes and updates. Most have correctly declared the winners for many years. They determine who the current winners are.

The AP may not announce a winner on election night. It may take a few days or even weeks to determine a winner. A winner is announced when the race callers are sure a candidate has won.

Other news media determine the winner a little differently. For example, the major TV networks use

News platforms cover election night differently. However, most show some sort of map to keep track of the counting of the votes.

Though a winner may be announced, election results aren't official until they are verified. This can take several weeks.

their own data. They also use exit polls to learn voter preferences. They may declare a winner earlier or later. Or they may declare a different winner altogether.

MAKING IT OFFICIAL

The outcome of the election is not official yet. The votes must be **canvassed** first. Then the results must be certified. These tasks may take several weeks following Election Day.

The canvass tallies all votes. It guarantees that each valid vote is part of the final results. An election official or group of officials reviews the results. They gather and verify every valid ballot. They find any discrepancies. They fix errors. They work to make sure the count is complete and accurate.

Sometimes votes need to be **audited**. This is a way of making sure that the results are correct. This is especially important because elections are computerized. Sometimes machines make errors. Auditing involves taking a small sample of the paper ballots. They are examined by hand. Then they are

Auditing votes by hand allows people to find any errors made by machines.

compared to the machine's results. This way, officials can be sure the machines recorded and counted the votes correctly.

Once the canvassing is complete, the election can be certified. Election officials confirm that the election results are true. This can take place from 1 to 3 days after the election. The amount of time states have to certify the election varies.

In a presidential election, certifying the election makes it clear who the electors should vote for. The electors are part of the Electoral College. They gather in their state capitols to cast their ballots. This is called the National Electoral Vote. Congress meets on January 6

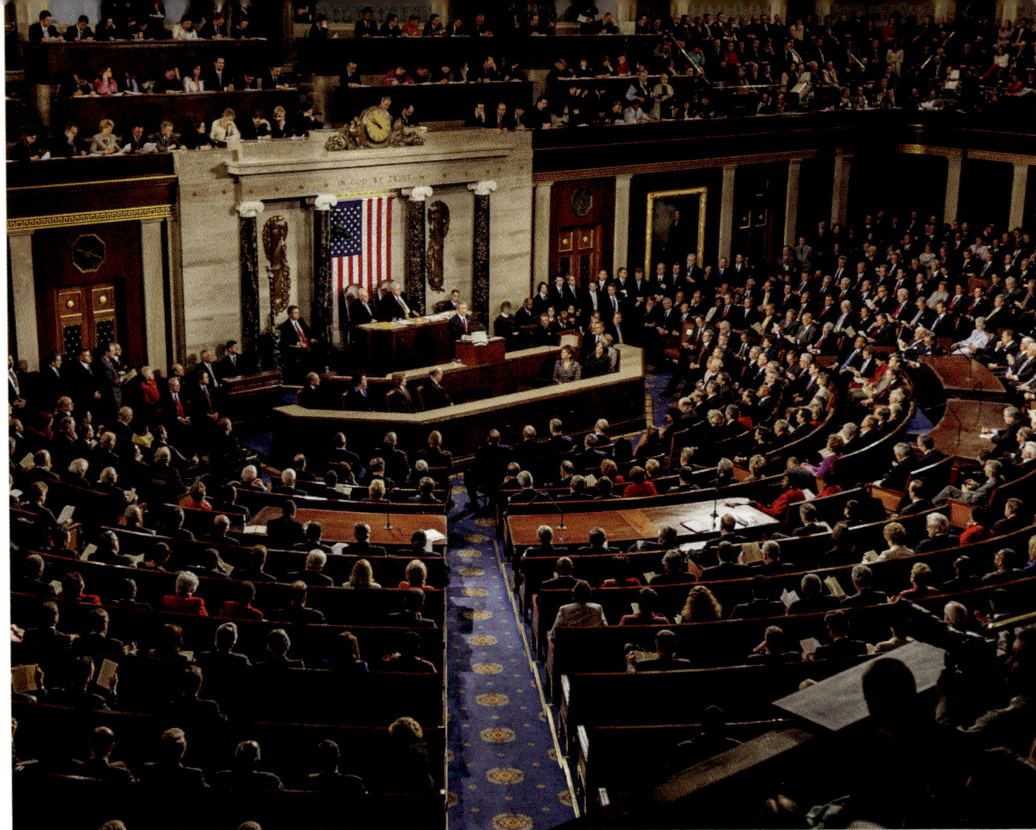

Members of the Senate and House of Representatives meet in a joint session on January 6 to officially count electoral votes.

to count the electoral votes. The candidate who receives 270 votes becomes the next president of the United States.

After the election, all paper ballots and records from the popular vote are securely stored in a sealed container. They stay there for at least 22 months. There is limited access for extra security. After enough time has passed, the ballots are destroyed.

FUN FACT: THE FIRST TUESDAY AFTER THE FIRST MONDAY

The date for Election Day was chosen for several different reasons. In 1845, many Americans were farmers. Holding the election in November avoided the harvest season. But there were other things to consider. Tuesday was chosen to avoid religious commitments. Some people had to travel a long way to vote. Voters who attended church on Sunday didn't want to miss it to vote on Monday. Lawmakers also did not want Election Day to fall on November 1. Merchants used that day to figure out their income from October. The first Tuesday after the first Monday solved that problem.

ACTIVITY

JOIN IN!

People must be 18 years old to vote. But younger people can get involved in elections too! Read through the list below. Find an activity you would like to try. Then ask your parent or another trusted adult to help you get started.

- Educate yourself. Stay informed about political issues, candidates, and the election process. With the help of a parent, teacher, or librarian, research news articles about the latest issues. Find out where your local representative stands on the issues. Do you agree with them? Why or why not?
- Attend a local political meeting. Find out when the next town hall or city council meeting will be held in your city. Attend the meeting with a parent or other trusted adult. In a notebook, write down the different issues discussed. Which issues do you think are the most important ones facing your city? Why?
- Volunteer with a campaign. Find a campaign in your area with a candidate you support. It can be a local, state, or national campaign. Volunteer to help with the campaign. Activities may include canvassing with other students and adults, stuffing envelopes, phone banking, or helping with a fundraiser or other event.

- Promote voter registration. Ask your school to host a voter registration drive. Volunteer to participate in the drive. Encourage your friends to participate too. Keep track of the number of registrations that came from your drive. Each one of those represents a new voter!
- Attend debates and forums. Go with a parent to a local debate or forum where candidates discuss their views. Take along a notebook and write down the issues that were discussed. At home, ask your parents how they feel about the issues. Do you agree or disagree? Why?
- Organize a mock election. Ask your teacher for permission to hold a mock election in class. As a class, choose two candidates who will compete for votes. Have the candidates give speeches about their stand on some issues at school. Using secret ballots, have the students choose the candidate they prefer. Your teacher can count and verify the ballots.
- Work at the polls. Most states allow students ages 16 and older to be regular poll workers. Check with your state or local government office to see how old you have to be to volunteer. Once you are eligible, sign up to help during the next election.

GLOSSARY

audited (AA-duht-id) examined and reviewed in a methodic manner

ballot (BA-luht) a piece of paper or electronic device on which people who are voting enter their choices

canvassed (KAN-vuhsd) counted to ensure every valid vote is included in final election results

cartridge (KAHR-trij) a removable electronic device that stores data

certified (SUR-tuh-fied) guaranteed the accuracy of something

eligible (E-luh-juh-buhl) qualified

interpreters (in-TUHR-pruh-tuhrz) people who translate for people communicating in different languages

jurisdiction (jur-uhs-DIK-shuhn) an area where an authority is exercised

manually (MAN-yoo-wuh-lee) doing something by hand without the use of machinery

monitor (MAH-nuh-tuhr) to watch or check on something

nonpartisan (NAAN-paar-tuh-zuhn) not affiliated with a political party

nonprofit (nahn-PRAH-fuht) a business or organization not established to make a profit

passport (PAS-port) an official document that allows citizens to travel to other countries

precinct (PREE-sinkt) an area in a town that forms a separate district for voting

tallying (ta-LEE-ing) finding the total of something

verified (VER-uh-fied) confirmed as accurate

TO LEARN MORE

BOOKS

Edwards, Sue Bradford. *Voting and Elections*. Lake Elmo, MN: Focus Readers, 2024.

Howard, Sherry. *Voting for President*. Huntington Beach, CA: Teacher Created Materials, 2022.

Smith, Erin Geiger. *Thank You for Voting: The Past, Present, and Future of Voting*. New York: Harper, 2020.

WEBSITES

Search these online sources with an adult:

"Life of a Ballot." NBC News.

"Student's Power: Elections." ICivics.com.

"The History and Process of Voting." Ben's Guide.

INDEX

ABOUT THE AUTHOR

Samantha Bell was born and raised near Orlando, Florida. She grew up in a family of eight kids and all kinds of pets, including goats, chickens, cats, dogs, rabbits, horses, parakeets, hamsters, guinea pigs, a monkey, a raccoon, and a coatimundi. She now lives with her family in the foothills of the Blue Ridge Mountains, where she enjoys hiking, painting, and snuggling with their cats, Pocket, Pebble, and Mr. Tree-Tree Triggers.